RUSES

ourne

H www.heinemann.co.uk/library

Visit our website to find out more information about **Heinemann Library** books.

To order:
- ☎ Phone 44 (0) 1865 888066
- 🖹 Send a fax to 44 (0) 1865 314091
- 💻 Visit the Heinemann Bookshop at www.heinemann.co.uk/library to browse our catalogue and order online.

First published in Great Britain by Heinemann Library, Halley Court, Jordan Hill, Oxford OX2 8EJ, part of Harcourt Education.

Heinemann is a registered trademark of Harcourt Education Ltd.

Editorial: Nancy Dickmann and Tanvi Rai
Design: Richard Parker and Celia Floyd
Illustrations: Art Construction
Picture Research: Rebecca Sodergren and Pete Morris
Production: Séverine Ribierre

Originated by Dot Gradations Ltd
Printed in China by WKT Company Limited

ISBN 0 431 17515 2 (hardback)
08 07 06 05 04
10 9 8 7 6 5 4 3 2 1

ISBN 0 431 17522 5 (paperback)
09 08 07 06 05
10 9 8 7 6 5 4 3 2 1

British Library Cataloguing in Publication Data
Claybourne, Anna
Microlife. – (Science Answers)
579
A full catalogue record for this book is available from the British Library.

Acknowledgements
The publishers would like to thank the following for permission to reproduce photographs: Getty images **p. 24**; Harcourt Education Ltd/Tudor Photography **pp. 15, 17, 23**; Science Photo Library/Petit Format/Institut Pasteur/Charles Daguet **p. 9**; Science Photo Library **p. 6, 27, 28**; Science Photo Library/A. B. Dowsett **p. 18**; Science Photo Library/Andrew Syred **pp. 16, 20**; Science Photo Library/David Munns **p. 22**; Science Photo Library/David Scharf **pp. 8, 14**; Science Photo Library/Doug Martin **p. 26**; Science Photo Library/Dr Tony Brain **p. 5**; Science Photo Library/Eye of Science **pp. 10, 25**; Science Photo Library/Kwangshin Kim **p. 4**; Science Photo Library/Martin F. Chillmaid **p. 11**; Science Photo Library/NASA **p. 13**; Science Photo Library/National Cancer Institute **p. 12**; Science Photo Library/Pascal Goetgheluck **p. 7**; Science Photo Library/St Mary's Hospital Medical School **p. 21**; SPL/Gilette Corporation **p. 29**.

Cover photograph of *Pseudomonas* bacteria on the lining of a human nose reproduced with permission of SPL/Juergen Bergen, Max Planck Institute.

Contents

Any words appearing in bold, **like this**, are explained in the Glossary.

About the experiments and demonstrations

This book contains some boxes headed 'Science Answers'. Each one describes an experiment or demonstration that you can try yourself. There are some simple safety rules to follow when doing an experiment:

- Ask an adult to help with any cutting using a sharp knife.
- After any experiment involving micro-organisms, wrap up all the disposable materials in a plastic bag and throw them away in a bin. Thoroughly wash your hands and any containers you have used.

Materials you will use

Most of the experiments and demonstrations in this book can be done with objects that you can find in your own home and food you can buy cheaply from a shop. You will also need a pencil and paper to record your results.

What is microlife?

Microlife is a general name given to tiny creatures called micro-organisms. The word 'micro' means very small, and '**organism**' means a living thing.

Micro-organisms are much smaller than other small creatures, such as ants and flies. In fact, they are too tiny to see without a **microscope**. Although you normally can't see them, there are millions of micro-organisms all around you. They live in water, in soil, in the air, in food and even on and inside our bodies.

Why do micro-organisms matter?

Micro-organisms are incredibly important – not just for humans, but for the whole planet. They feed on other living things that have died, helping to **recycle** chemicals back into the soil. They help our bodies to work. We also use different kinds of micro-organisms to make chemicals, medicines and foods, such as bread, cheese and yoghurt.

At the same time, some micro-organisms can create problems. They can cause diseases that harm people, animals and crops. They can make our food go off, rot our teeth and make water supplies, kitchens and hospitals dirty and unhealthy.

Sometimes dangerous?

The micro-organism in this picture is a type of **bacteria** called *Escherichia coli*, shown through a microscope. It lives in human **intestines**, and is usually harmless. However, some types of *E. coli* can give you a bad stomach upset if you swallow them.

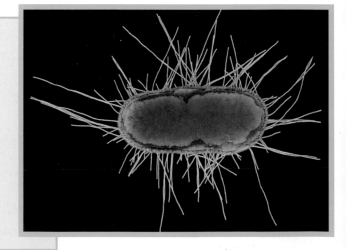

How big is a micro-organism?

Micro-organisms are all small, but they come in a range of different sizes. A typical bacterium, like the *E. coli* shown on page 4, measures about one **micron** across. A micron is one thousandth of a millimetre. That means you could fit about 250,000 *E. coli* bacteria on the full stop at the end of this sentence.

But a single bacterium is big compared to a **virus**, the smallest kind of micro-organism. A typical virus is only one-thousandth the size of an *E. coli* bacterium. You could fit 250 million of them on to a full stop.

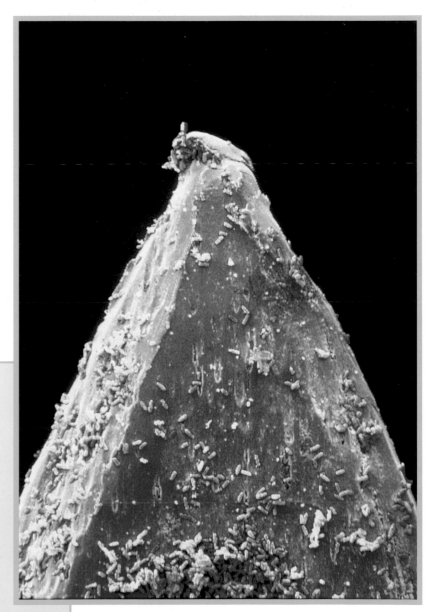

Magnified micro-organisms

In this magnified photo you can see rod-shaped bacteria (orange) on the tip of a syringe needle, hundreds of times bigger than they are in real life.

How were micro-organisms discovered?

We have only known about micro-organisms for around 350 years. This is because they could only be seen once we had microscopes. The first microscopes were invented in around 1600, and by the 1650s they were powerful enough to show larger micro-organisms, such as bacteria.

One of the first people to see micro-organisms was Dutchman Anton van Leeuwenhoek (1632-1723). In a scientific experiment in 1683, he took some **plaque** from the teeth of two old men who had never cleaned their teeth. Under a microscope, van Leeuwenhoek saw tiny bacteria swimming and wriggling around. He called them 'animalcules'. Over the next 200 years, microscopes got better and better, so more micro-organisms were discovered and named.

Scientific discoveries

In the 19th century, scientists such as Joseph Lister, shown here at his microscope, and Louis Pasteur (see page 28), realized that some micro-organisms could **infect** wounds and cause diseases.

More names for micro-organisms

Like other living things, most **species** (types) of micro-organisms also have their own scientific names. For example, the bacteria that causes the deadly disease **anthrax** is called *Bacillus anthracis*, or *B. anthracis* for short. Scientific names like this are usually in Latin, and are written in italics. People also use general names for micro-organisms, such as 'germs' or 'bugs'.

Looking at micro-organisms

The first microscopes used glass lenses, like those used in magnifying glasses, to magnify objects (make them look bigger). Some microscopes still work this way, including the light microscopes often used in classrooms. Today, the most powerful modern microscopes are huge, expensive **scanning electron microscopes**. They work by firing tiny **particles**, called **electrons**, at a microscopic object. When the electrons bounce back, they form a pattern. A computer turns this pattern into a picture and displays it on a computer screen. Most of the pictures of micro-organisms in this book were taken using a scanning electron microscope. The pictures are black and white to start with and have colour added afterwards to make them clearer.

What kinds of micro-organisms are there?

Many micro-organisms are single-celled, which means they have just one **cell** each. Cells are the building blocks of all living things. The human body, for example, is made up of around 50 million million cells. Each cell is too tiny to be seen on its own. So, as you can imagine, one cell is very small indeed.

Micro-organisms can be divided into several main groups. These are:
- **bacteria** – tiny creatures that are not plants or animals
- **viruses** – the smallest micro-organisms of all
- **algae** – single-celled creatures related to plants
- **protozoa** – single-celled creatures similar to tiny animals
- **fungi** and **moulds** – single-celled micro-organisms related to mushrooms.

What is a bacterium?

A bacterium is a very common type of micro-organism. Bacteria have only one cell each, and they are often round or sausage-shaped. Some types of bacteria can cause diseases, but most of them are harmless or even useful. They are an important part of soil, and are found in many other places, too. This image shows bacteria on a kitchen scrub pad!

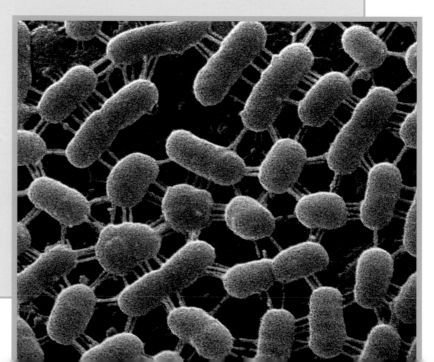

Some types of very small multi-celled creatures, such as nematode worms, which live in the soil and other places, are also called micro-organisms because they can only be seen with a microscope.

Are viruses alive?

Viruses, which are the smallest micro-organisms, are unusual because they are not made of cells. A virus is much smaller than a cell. Some scientists say viruses are not really living things at all, as they do not eat or breathe, and cannot **breed** on their own. Instead, a virus works by attacking a cell and using the cell to make copies of itself. Viruses are so tiny, they can breed inside bacteria and other cells. The flu and the common cold are examples of diseases caused by viruses. This series of pictures shows a HIV virus (which can cause **AIDS**) invading a human cell.

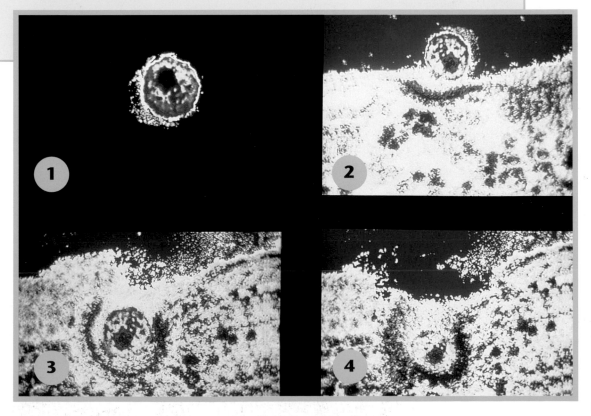

More micro-organisms

Besides bacteria and viruses, micro-organisms include single-celled plants and tiny animal-like creatures. Algae are like tiny plants. They float in water or grow on damp surfaces, such as paving stones. Like other plants, they need sunlight to survive. Although one alga is too small to see except through a microscope, you can sometimes see a greenish tinge in a pond or fish tank where millions of algae are living. Just like larger plants, algae give off **oxygen** as they feed.

Fungi grow on rotting fruit and vegetables, or on living things. For example, athlete's foot, which grows on people's feet, is a type of fungi. So is **yeast**, which we use to make bread rise. Moulds include things like the black mould that grows in damp bathrooms and the jelly-like slime that sometimes grows on grass. You can see these things because you're looking at thousands of millions of micro-organisms all growing together in a group. Each individual micro-organism is too small to see on its own.

Single-celled animals

Protozoa are like very small animals, usually made up of just one cell. They can move around by stretching and shrinking themselves, or by waving tiny hairs or finger shapes on their bodies. Some protozoa cause diseases, such as **malaria** and **giardia**. Here, malaria protozoa (yellow) are seen bursting out of human red blood cells.

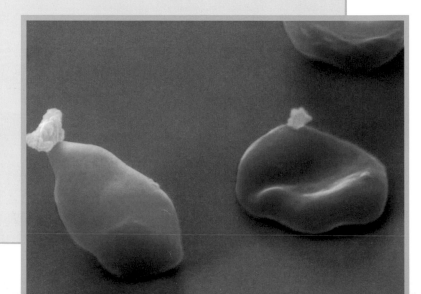

Living together

Many types of micro-organisms, such as algae, bacteria, yeast and slime moulds, live together in big groups called **colonies**. The colony grows as the micro-organisms breed and multiply into a bigger and bigger mass. Although they can't talk to each other like we do, scientists think the micro-organisms in a colony may be able to send each other messages using chemicals.

A yeast colony

This block of yeast is made up of a mass of millions of single-celled creatures. Are they all communicating with each other using chemical signals?

Where are micro-organisms found?

Micro-organisms are found in most places. Soil is full of **bacteria**, **algae**, worms and other microscopic animals. Other bacteria, **viruses** and **protozoa** live in or on larger living things, such as plants, animals and people. In a typical house, there are bacteria in food, on damp cloths, on door handles, on telephone handsets and on anything else that people touch. **Fungi** live on rotten fruit and bread, around baths and toilets and in damp corners.

At home in the heat

Some amazing bacteria, called **thermophilic** bacteria, like to live in boiling hot water. They are found around **hydrothermal vents**, where hot springs bubble up from cracks in the seabed. They feed on **minerals** in the water.

Dangerous water

Water usually contains some micro-organisms. Algae and protozoa float in the sea and in river and pond water. The drinking water that comes out of our taps also contains a few harmless bacteria. But in some parts of the world, drinking water may contain micro-organisms that cause serious diseases, like cholera, dysentery or **bilharzia**. Bilharzia is caused by the tiny bilharzia flatworm (shown here). If people bathe in or drink infected water it can make them very ill, or even kill them.

How do micro-organisms move from place to place?

Micro-organisms need to move around to find food and places to live, but only a few of them can move by themselves. Protozoa and worms can swim or crawl along, but bacteria, algae, fungi and viruses usually just float around. They get spread from place to place by wind, water or by other living things. For example, a bacterium in the air could land on a leaf, which could by eaten by a cow. The bacterium could then grow and breed into many bacteria in the cow's body. Some of the bacteria might leave the cow's body in its dung and land in the soil, or get in to the cow's milk and end up in your fridge, and so on. Some viruses, such as the common cold virus, can spread from one person to another when they cough or sneeze.

Are there micro-organisms in space?

Some scientists think there is evidence that a type of small bacteria-like micro-organism once lived on the planet Mars. If they are right, this will be the first life ever discovered beyond our planet. This tube-like structure (blue) was found on a meteorite that came from Mars.

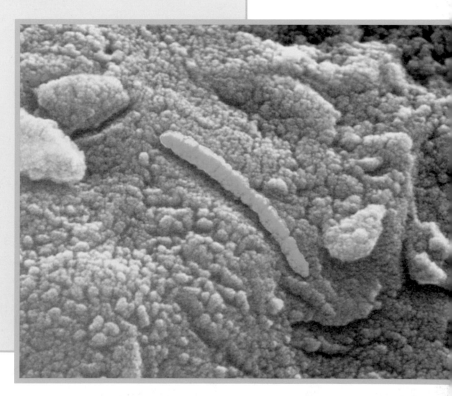

Where are most micro-organisms?

Like other living things, most micro-organisms find it easiest to survive in warm, damp places where there is plenty of food and water. So, there isn't much microlife in the sands of a hot, dry desert, or the ice at the top of a mountain, but there are huge numbers in soft, damp soil. One handful of soil can contain up to six billion bacteria. That is almost as many human beings as there are on the Earth.

It's the same in our homes. The biggest numbers of micro-organisms are found in warm, damp places, such as a pan of soup that's been left out on a warm day. In these conditions, any bacteria in the soup will be able to keep feeding and **breeding** until there are millions and millions of them. The human body is a perfect home for micro-organisms, too. Fungi can live on your skin, and viruses can invade your body and give you diseases. But the busiest part of your body is your **large intestine**, which is home to billions of bacteria.

At home in the soil

The *Bacillus* bacteria shown here live in huge numbers in the soil. Warm, moist soil provides all the food and warmth these micro-organisms require. They feed on dead and decaying **organic matter**.

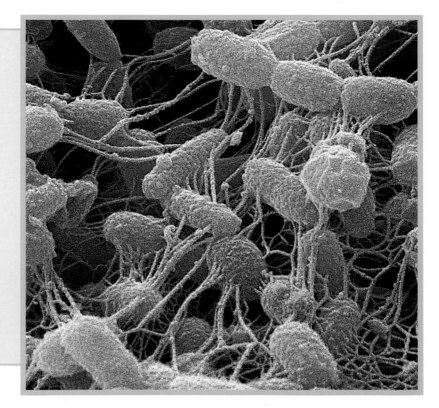

EXPERIMENT: Does milk go off faster in or out of the fridge?

HYPOTHESIS:
Milk will go off faster if it's kept warm, because the bacteria in it will breed faster.

EQUIPMENT:
A carton of fresh milk, two identical glasses, a refrigerator, a pen and paper.

EXPERIMENT STEPS:
1 Pour some milk into each glass. Put one glass of milk in the fridge and the other somewhere warm, such as a sunny windowsill or a shelf over a heater.
2 On a piece of paper, describe how the milk in each glass looks and smells. Then, at the same time every day, examine the glasses again and write down how the milk looks and smells. Continue the experiment for up to 3 days. When it's finished, throw the milk away.
3 Write down what you saw.

CONCLUSION:
The milk that's kept warm changes much faster than the milk that's kept cold. It starts to smell sour and look lumpy. This is because the bacteria in it can breed much faster in the warm temperatures, so the milk goes off. The milk in the fridge will take much longer to go off, because the bacteria breed much more slowly in the cold.

How do micro-organisms live?

Like other living things, most micro-organisms need a supply of food and **moisture** to keep them alive. Many also need **oxygen**, although a few types of **bacteria** do not need oxygen to survive. Many need sunlight, too. When they have everything they need, micro-organisms can grow and **reproduce**.

What do micro-organisms eat?

Just like us, most organisms feed on **organic matter** – other living things or living things that have died. For example, the bacteria that live on our teeth eat sugar from the food we put in our mouths. **Mould** growing on bread feeds on the bread, and **yeast** feeds on the sugary chemicals found in some foods. Some bacteria, such as *Streptococcus pyogenes*, eat living flesh. **Algae** and some types of bacteria are like plants – they feed by turning sunlight into energy. Some micro-organisms eat other micro-organisms.

Eating without mouths

Most micro-organisms don't have mouths. They eat by soaking up food through their skin or, like this amoeba (green), by wrapping themselves around food particles.

Why are viruses different?

Unlike other micro-organisms, **viruses** don't eat, breathe or grow. Instead, they simply **replicate**, or copy themselves. They do this using materials from the **cells** of other living things, so they never need to eat. You can see how this works on page 19.

EXPERIMENT: Make a mould garden

HYPOTHESIS:
Moulds will grow on most foods at room temperature. Some foods will go mouldy more quickly than others.

EQUIPMENT:
A large, clear, lidded glass or plastic container or jar that can be thrown away after the experiment; different kinds of food, such as fruit, bread, cake, cheese and crisps; paper and pen.

EXPERIMENT STEPS:
1 Wash out the container.
2 Take each piece of food and dip it in water.
3 Put all the food in the container and put the lid on.
4 Leave the container in a well-lit place at room temperature.
5 As the food starts to go mouldy, describe and draw what you see. Check the food every day.
6 Write down what you saw.

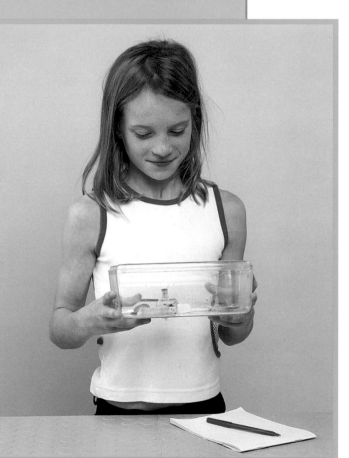

CONCLUSION:
After a few days, you will see mould and **fungi** starting to grow. Different types of mould will grow on different foods. Do some foods take longer than others to go mouldy? This is partly because some prepackaged foods, such as crisps, contain preservatives – chemicals that make it harder for mould to grow.

How do micro-organisms reproduce?

Reproducing means **breeding**, or having babies. Although micro-organisms don't have babies in the same way that humans do, they do breed and make copies of themselves. **Protozoa** often do this by simply splitting in two. Some types of fungi release **spores**, which are like tiny seeds. They float away in the air and may grow into new fungi wherever they land. Worms lay eggs, which grow into new worms.

How do bacteria breed?

Most bacteria reproduce by dividing. To make new bacteria, a single-celled bacterium grows bigger and bigger, and makes a copy of its **genes** – the instructions inside it that make it work. Then it separates into two new cells, each with its own copy of the genes. The two new bacteria are copies of the first bacteria and are called daughter cells.

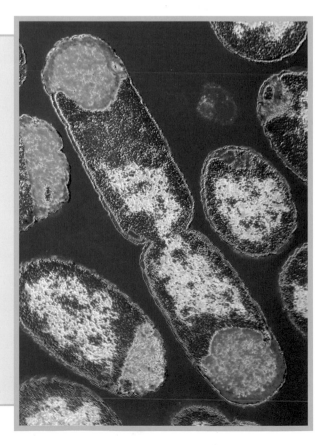

Microlife multiplication

Micro-organisms such as bacteria, which divide by splitting in two, can breed very fast. Each new bacterium divides into two more, and each of those divides into two more, and so on, causing a bacteria population explosion. *Escherichia coli* bacteria, for example, can divide every 20 minutes. At this rate, as long as there is enough food and moisture, one *E. coli* bacterium can turn into more than a million bacteria in just 7 hours.

How do viruses replicate?

Viruses can only replicate by invading another cell, such as a bacterium, or an animal's body cell. A virus contains a set of instructions for making copies of itself (genes). The virus replicates itself by forcing a cell to follow these instructions. Here is how it works:

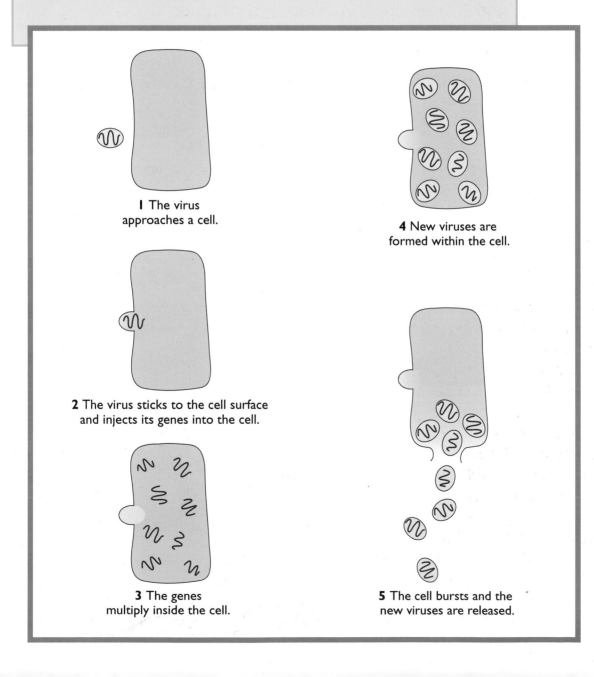

I The virus approaches a cell.

4 New viruses are formed within the cell.

2 The virus sticks to the cell surface and injects its genes into the cell.

3 The genes multiply inside the cell.

5 The cell bursts and the new viruses are released.

How do micro-organisms help us?

Some people think of 'germs' and 'bugs' as bad or dirty, but in fact many types of micro-organisms are essential to life on Earth. The most important job micro-organisms do is to make things rot. When a plant or animal dies and **decays**, what is actually happening is that it is being eaten by **bacteria**, worms, **fungi** or other micro-organisms. They break down the chemicals in things that have died and **recycle** them back into the soil. These chemicals then help plants to grow, making new food for other living things. If micro-organisms didn't do this, dead plants and animals would never decay. They would just pile up on the Earth's surface.

How do micro-organisms help our bodies?

Many of the billions of bacteria living inside you are very good for you. For example, *Bifidobacteria* in your **large intestine** make **vitamins** that help your body, while *Lactobacillus bulgaricus* (visible here as long, pink strands in natural yoghurt) guard your **intestines** against other bacteria that can cause diseases.

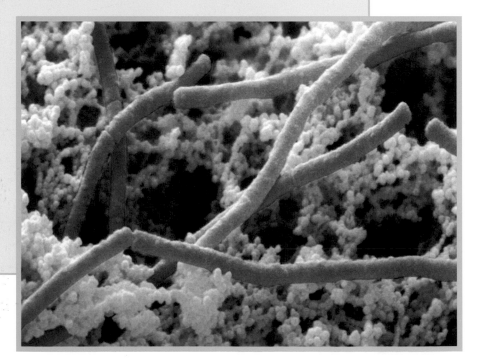

How do micro-organisms help animals eat?

Micro-organisms also help to **digest** and break down the food we eat. This is even more important for animals such as cows, because the foods they eat, such as grasses, are very hard to digest. A cow's **rumen**, or stomach, is full of bacteria and **protozoa** that can break down tough grasses and turn them into chemicals, which the cow's body uses to grow and to make milk.

How did Fleming discover antibiotics?

In 1929, British scientist Alexander Fleming discovered that a type of **mould**, growing on an unwashed dish in his lab, seemed to be able to kill deadly disease-causing bacteria. He realized that the mould, called *Penicillium*, was releasing some chemicals that were destroying the bacteria. These useful chemicals, which were later found to be made by various types of micro-organisms, are now known as **antibiotics**. They are often used to treat illnesses and **infections** caused by bacteria.

What do we use micro-organisms for?

As well as being useful in the natural world, micro-organisms are used in factories and homes to make foods such as bread, beer, cheese and yoghurt. Over thousands of years, humans have discovered that certain micro-organisms give food tastes and textures we like. For example, when **yeast** feeds on sugar, it gives off bubbles of carbon dioxide gas, which give bread dough a soft, spongy texture as it bakes.

There are many other products besides food that contain micro-organisms or the chemicals they make. For example, some types of washing powder contain chemicals called **enzymes**, which help to destroy stains on clothes. They are made by types of bacteria, which are found naturally in soil. Micro-organisms are also used to make medicines, to kill insect pests, and to process **sewage** and other waste.

Using micro-organisms with milk

Bacteria are used to turn milk into yoghurt. Cheeses such as Roquefort (seen here) and Blue Stilton contain bluish-green moulds, which are added to the cheese to give it a tangy taste.

EXPERIMENT: What does yeast feed on?

HYPOTHESIS:
Yeast will feed on sugar and make bubbles of gas as a waste product.

EQUIPMENT:
2 sachets of dried yeast, 2 small bowls, a teaspoon and a cup, granulated sugar, warm water, paper and pen.

EXPERIMENT STEPS:
1 Put a cupful of warm (not hot) water and the contents of a sachet of yeast into each bowl and stir.
2 Add a teaspoonful of sugar to one bowl and stir.
3 Put both bowls in a warm place, such as over a heater.
4 After 10 minutes, write down what has happened.

CONCLUSION:
The yeast with sugar added will produce lots of bubbles as it feeds on the sugar. They appear as a foam on top of the water. When the yeast has no sugar to feed on, it makes hardly any bubbles.

How do micro-organisms harm us?

While some micro-organisms are useful, others are a big nuisance for humans, and can even be deadly. They can cause diseases, make food go bad and destroy crops. Micro-organisms that cause diseases are often called pathogens. They include many types of **bacteria**, which can cause diseases such as sore throats, **TB** (**tuberculosis**) and **meningitis**. **Viruses** cause colds and flu, as well as **AIDS** and many other serious diseases. **Protozoa** cause **malaria** and **bilharzia**, which often make people ill in hot countries. Bacteria and **fungi** can get into wounds and cause blood poisoning or gangrene, which makes flesh rot away.

How do germs cause diseases?

Germs often cause diseases because they make waste chemicals that are bad for your body, or because the way they reproduce and feed damages your cells. Germs infect us because our bodies provide them with the warmth, **moisture** and food they need to survive. The illnesses they cause are just a side-effect. The person shown here is suffering from a common cold, caused by a virus.

Rotting food

It's natural for meat, vegetables and other food to **decay** over time – but this causes a problem when we want to store food or transport it long distances. If food goes off and contains a lot of bacteria, it tastes bad and can make you ill.

What do bacteria do to teeth?

Teeth make a good home for bacteria such as *Streptococcus mutans*. There are lots of nooks and crannies for them to hide in, and lots of food constantly passing by for them to eat. Unfortunately for us, when they feed on sugar, these bacteria produce an acid that eats away at teeth, making them decay. Brushing your teeth to clean away the **plaque** (shown here as a yellow coating on the tooth surface) helps to stop them decaying.

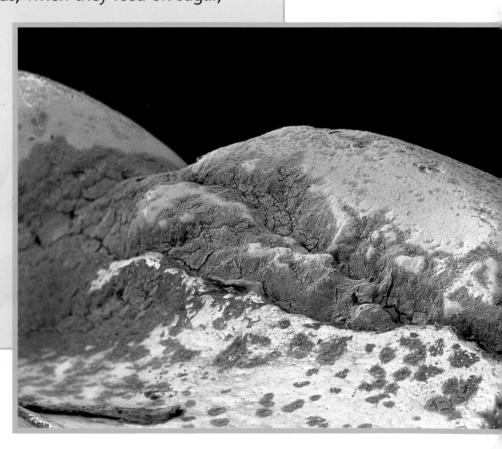

How can we fight germs?

Your body has an **immune system** designed to fight off most everyday germs. Scientists have also discovered many medicines and treatments that kill disease germs or keep them under control. We can keep germs at bay by cleaning kitchens, bathrooms, food factories and hospitals with germ-killing chemicals, such as bleach. Keeping food in the fridge or freezer, or making sure it's thoroughly cooked, makes it harder for bugs to **breed**. Washing your hands after you go to the toilet helps you to avoid germs too.

Creating a barrier

One of the best ways to keep germs out of the places we don't want them is by using what is called the barrier method. This means that a barrier is created between a possible source of germs and the thing we want to keep sterile (free from germs). This is why nurses and doctors wear gloves, gowns and masks during operations, and why people who prepare and serve food wear gloves and caps.

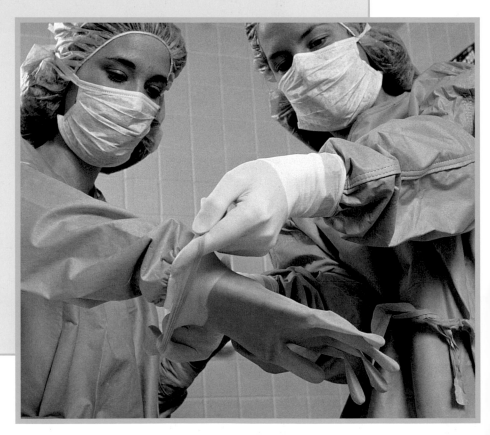

Do micro-organisms harm plants and animals?

Just like humans, plants and animals can catch diseases and infections caused by micro-organisms. In fact, many micro-organisms only affect a particular **species**. For example, cat flu is caused by three different viruses which only affect cats. Micro-organisms can harm wildlife, too. Hundreds of gorillas in Africa have died after catching the deadly **ebola** virus.

Trouble for farmers

Micro-organisms can be a big problem for farmers. Fungi and viruses can damage crop plants like potatoes and coffee. The picture below shows a lettuce damaged by a fungus called Sclerotinia. Farm animals, such as cows and sheep, can get diseases like scrapie, nagana and **anthrax**, which are caused by micro-organisms and can be fatal. When germs kill farm crops or animals, they also harm people, as it affects their food supply and can even cause a **famine**. This happened in Ireland in the 1840s, when a fungus that attacked potatoes spread across the country. Millions of people went short of food, and up to a million of them died of hunger.

People who found the answers

Ignatz Semmelweiss (1818-65)

Semmelweiss was a doctor in a hospital in Vienna, Austria in the 1840s. He ran two **maternity wards** – one staffed by **midwives**, and one staffed by doctors who also worked in other wards. He noticed that in the doctors' ward, mothers were much more likely to catch **infections** and die in childbirth. He realized that the doctors must be spreading germs to the maternity ward from other parts of the hospital. By making the doctors wash their hands after seeing each patient, and change their clothes after operations, he massively reduced the rate of infection. The doctors were so angry about the new rules that Semmelweiss was fired and sent to a lunatic asylum, but his methods were soon adopted in other hospitals and are still important today.

Louis Pasteur (1822-95)

Before the 19th century, many people thought that micro-organisms grew by themselves out of non-living matter such as mud or water. In the 1860s, Louis Pasteur, a French scientist, proved that this was not true. He showed that micro-organisms could spread from one place to another in the air, and that they could **breed**, cause diseases and make food go off. His work led to major advances in medicine and food preparation. **Pasteurized** milk, for example, is named after Louis Pasteur. It is milk that has been heated to kill some of the **bacteria** it contains.

Amazing facts

- Experts think there may be as many as 10 million different **species** of micro-organisms, although they have not all been discovered and named. There are probably more different species of micro-organisms than there are species of all other living things put together.

- The **protozoan** that causes **malaria** is the most dangerous living thing ever – at least for humans. Malaria has killed more people than any other disease.

- **Infectious** diseases caused by micro-organisms kill about 17 million people per year around the world.

- Micro-organisms were the first living things to exist on Earth. It's thought they first developed in mud or water about 3.5 billion (3,500,000,000) years ago.

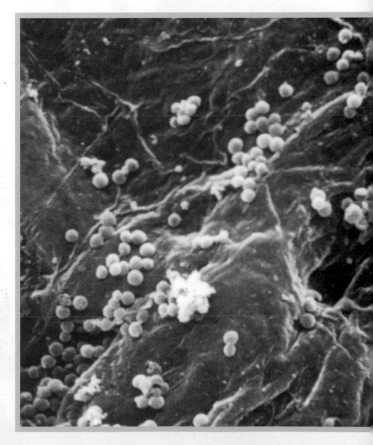

- One square centimetre of your skin has around 10 million micro-organisms living on it. They especially like warm, damp skin, like the skin between your toes or around your nose. Shown here is a picture of bacteria on skin, taken by a **scanning electron microscope**.

# Glossary

AIDS (short for Auto-Immune Deficiency Syndrome) disease that damages the body's immune system

algae tiny single-celled plants

anthrax disease spread by a bacterium, which both animals and people can catch

antibiotics chemicals that fight bacteria. They can be made by some types of moulds.

bacteria very common type of single-celled micro-organism

bilharzia disease carried by a protozoan that lives in water

breed to reproduce, or have babies

cells tiny units. Living things are made up of cells.

colony group of organisms that live together

decay to rot away

digest when your body breaks down food into useful chemicals that give you energy

ebola disease that causes bleeding inside the body. It is caused by a virus.

electron tiny particle. Electrons are part of the atoms that all substances are made up of.

enzyme type of chemical made by living things such as bacteria

famine widespread food shortage

fungus (plural **fungi**) type of living thing such as yeasts, mushrooms and toadstools

genes instructions inside living things that tell them how to develop and survive

giardia disease spread by protozoa sometimes found in water supplies in hot countries

hydrothermal vent crack in the seabed that releases hot water from inside the Earth

infect to get in to something and start to breed

infection illness or other problem caused by germs infecting something

infectious easily passed on from one person to another, for example by sneezing

immune system set of organs and cells in your body that work together to fight dangerous germs

intestines tubes inside your body that soak up useful chemicals from the food you eat and carry any waste out of your body

large intestine widest section of your intestines, which holds waste

malaria disease caused by a protozoan that is spread from one person to another by mosquitoes

maternity ward hospital ward where women go to give birth to their babies

meningitis disease that affects the skin-like layers surrounding the brain

micron 1/1000 (a thousandth) of a millimetre, or 0.00004 inches

microscope machine that magnifies objects (makes them look bigger)

midwife someone whose job is to help women give birth to their babies

minerals non-living substances the Earth is made of, such as rocks and metals

moisture another word for water, wetness or dampness

mould type of micro-organism that grows on food and in damp corners

organic matter substances that are alive or were once alive, such as plants, meat and wood

organism another name for a living thing

oxygen gas found in the air. Most living things need it in order to survive.

particle tiny piece or part of something

pasteurize to heat milk or other food in order to kill the micro-organisms in it

plaque mixture of bacteria, food and acid that grows on your teeth

protozoa tiny single-celled animals

recycle change something old into a new form so it can be used again

replicate make exact copies of itself

reproduce to breed, or have babies

rumen stomach of a cow or other grass-eating animal such as a deer

scanning electron miscroscope type of very powerful microscope

sewage human waste from toilets and sinks

species scientific name for a type of living thing

spores tiny seed-like objects that some fungi and moulds use to reproduce

TB (tuberculosis) disease that can affect the lungs and bones

thermophilic able to survive at high temperatures

virus type of tiny micro-organism that survives by invading the cells of living things

vitamins useful chemicals that help your body to work

yeast type of fungus used to make bread, beer and other foods

Index

More books to read

Hidden Life Series, Andrew Solway (Heinemann Library, 2004)
Microlife: A world of micro-organisms, Robert Snedden
    (Heinemann Library, 2000)
Nature Encyclopedia (Dorling Kindersley, 1998)